The Secret Code of Girls

Empowering Girls to Mature into Confident Women

Mae Dixon

Published by

MAE Dixon, LLC

P O Box 626

Largo, FL 33779-0626

maedixon62@gmail.com

Other publications at MaeDixon.com

Request permission must be in writing to maedixon62@gmail.com

First edition published 2017

ISBN - 978-1-7353725-0-1

ISBN – 978-17353725-1-8

Printed in The United States

MAE Dixon, LLC

DEDICATION

This book is dedicated to my granddaughters and all of the "girls" whose lives I've been blessed to impact in some small way over the years.

CONTENTS

ACKNOWLEDGEMENTS

I have wished so many times that I had known the contents of this book when I was a little girl. My maternal grandparents died before I was born, and I never got to know my paternal grandparents. My mother's mom died when she was a little girl, and since she and her siblings were left to raise themselves in a very closed environment, a lot of mistakes were made. In turn, my mother and her siblings did their best to raise their own children to be God-fearing, hardworking, and loving human beings.

I was blessed to have two sons, Calvin and Demetrius. They gave me seven granddaughters to whom I dedicate this book. It was being around these girls, goddaughters, and the young ladies that I've mentored that I learned how to be a girl—if you can imagine a girly-girl at age 60+.

I would like to give a big thanks to my mom, who is now deceased, for the sacrifices she made to give me life and teach me that I could be anything that I wanted to be. I am thankful for my father. He was in my life for only a short while, but he taught me how to be strong despite the odds and to understand a father's love. I am thankful for my brother Milton because he loves me and encourages me to be the leader that I am today. I would like to thank my sisters: Nina, who showed me what a survivor looks like, is my nurturer, sister, and friend; and Freda, my younger sister, makes me think that I can do anything. Another big thanks to Mrs. Julia Bell, China Reed (deceased), and Georgena Sanchez – Kizzy, who instilled in me the true meaning of becoming a woman of purpose. They supported me as surrogate mothers and friends. I am also thankful for my BFFs from middle school to now Jackie Wilson, Rosita Robsono, Jackie Gray, and China Hall; Shawn McCorkle, a colleague turned BFF of more than 20 years; and to all of my Sister-Friends of A Will & Way, Inc. who have helped to shape my life over the years.

Thanks to everyone who had a hand in the proofing of this book including Georgena Sanchez, Shawn McCorkle, Rosemary Lee Potter, and Kia and Moiya Dixon.

FOREWORD

By Mamie Webb Hixon

*T*he *Secret Code of Girls* is a how-to book. The *Secret Code of Girls* is an inspirational book designed to be a secret code for girls written by a "girl," whose secret codes about life and living have influenced many a girl in the communities in which she has lived and had influence. These girls range literally from ages 8 to 80, with, of course, the book's primary focus being on pre-teens and developing young adults, whose lives have similar emotional, social, and intellectual growth patterns. The book offers richness of material for any reader – the girl herself or the girl's parent(s). It' a guide for the college-bound girl, to the Kardashian wannabe, to the Beyonce look-alike, to the Michelle Obama girl, to the at-risk girl.

The book's how-to-ness derives from its "codes" on dating, coping, getting educated, and living with purpose. The book's inspiration derives from its imbedded timeliness and vison for a broader and brighter future for girls aspiring to be greater, and smarter in, their own right. The large and larger questions of personal, social, and familial responsibilities voiced by live girls alive with often difficult but inspiring dilemmas that the book addresses.

The *Secret Code* was conceived in school and church classrooms and other community venues where girls came together to ask and learn about life and living – before, during, and after girlhood. The learned messages have left the classrooms and other learning environments to reside on the pages of this book that girls can turn to for counsel, guidance, and leadership.

I can recall being a facilitator for one of these "girl classes," where confused girls, anxious and angry girls, silent and passive girls – all with muted voices – were reluctant and inhibited about sharing who they are and what they needed to know. Having had experience being one of those girls and having experienced communicating with those girls as an adult, the author is able to provide not only realistic questions but also reasonable answers for the girls in her book audience.

Without sermonizing or proselytizing, the text walks every young girl through a spatial, social, and emotional journey where family, leadership, civic engagement, volunteerism, and education take centerstage. Before "mentoring" became a viable buzzword, *The Secret Code* had originated in the mind of its author who wanted to tell girls' stories, share girls' lives, and motivate girls to become ladies and women.

The *Secret Code* allows girls to curl up on a couch or chaise lounge and become debutantes learning the codes of friendships, relationships, and kinships – no acts and scenes, no drama, no lip synching. Just words and secret codes for girls and secret codes of girls. All that's required is time to read and learn; time to think, reflect, and share; and time to enjoy being a girl.

INTRODUCTION

"**T**his book is the instructional guide for every girl entering puberty and beyond. For fathers who seek to understand and bond more with their daughters, this book is for you. Mothers who are raising sons and hope to one day have grandchildren, should gift this book to your son(s), after reading it yourselves, of course. It will help your son(s) understand girls/women better and to make a good choice when choosing a wife.

Every young girl needs this book to prepare them for a life of success and well-being. Invest in the gift of a lifetime. The wisdom gleaned from these pages will pay off many times during their lifetime.

CHAPTER ONE

Why Am
I Here

*E*ach one of us is born with a purpose. There are no acci-
dental births. You represent Love. As a living soul, you
are equipped to share with the world a gift that is unique to
you; that gift may be a skill, an emotion, a mere presence, or a
combination of them all.

While others may define you based on what they see or feel,
only you know innately what your true gifts are. There are
times when our gift(s) may overwhelm us because we don't feel
qualified, but just as we learn to walk and talk, as we mature

and learn to embrace the unique being that we are, our gift(s) becomes obvious, and we are then empowered to live it (them).

The knowing of why we're here may take a lifetime - meaning that by the time we recognize or accept our purpose, our life may be at its end. As humans, many of us fail to realize our value, and thus, we live life seeking what we already have within ourselves. Everything that we need to survive is built into the core of who we are. Public perception dictates that it is outward, that it's in the things that we accumulate, the relationships that we engage in, or our achievements, conquests, and victories.

"This above all: to thine own self be true, and it must follow, as the night the day, Thou canst not then be false to any man." This quote by William Shakespeare is a reminder that it's only when we take the time to know or learn ourselves that we're able to be authentic with others. When we fail to learn who we are, we're forced to rely on others to define us, and if we're not careful, this can lead to our demise. It is in this area that we lose ourselves because different people will see us differently; their perception will be based upon their own needs and not that of our own. If we're fortunate, the people who we allow to mold our lives will do so from a place of unconditional love and not from a place of selfish or deviant motives.

As a young person, it is difficult enough to live from day to day and therefore. It becomes necessary to check in with our core, our inner compass, our true self regularly. We know it as our Conscious; it is a Higher Power, the Creator of Truth. When we acknowledge and rely upon this Power within, we then become the person that we are destined to be and with fewer mistakes along the way.

Why A Girl?

Why not a girl? A girl is described in scripture as being the weaker vessel. A girl is also defined as a delicate creature. A girl is special; though you may be described as the weaker vessel, you are strong, delicate, and compassionate; you're wise and creative. As you grow into adulthood, you have the capacity for even greater possibilities. A girl is a female being.

CHAPTER TWO

THE FEMALE BODY

> *"Confidence is the sexiest attribute a woman can have. If you feel good, you'll look good." -Unknown*

The female body is indeed unique. While we, as girls, generally will all have the same parts, they will differ in size, color, and texture. It is important to note that we should become familiar with each part and give it the proper care. Don't be afraid to touch your body. Get to know how it feels so that when or if changes occur, you will know it. Keep your body clean inside and out; eat and drink responsibly and bathe regularly. Washing your face and brushing your teeth are tasks you should do every morning upon waking and every night before going to bed. A more detailed list of ways to care for your body is listed below.

The female body evolves as we mature; some of us are gifted with the ability to experience childbirth. Many things will happen within our bodies before we get to this stage. Mistakes can occur if we become emotionally mature without the benefit of wisdom. One of the reasons for this book is to help you to prepare for the different seasons of a girl's life. The menstrual cycle is a natural progression to womanhood and, for most, will come by surprise and should be welcomed. It is necessary for the female body to function properly. However, this process will now begin to occur for several days each month and will require you to be prepared for its monthly visit. You should have on hand special supplies (sanitary napkins, tampons, etc.) to protect your clothing.

As the body matures, it becomes susceptible to disease and infections which is why it is important and necessary to keep it clean and free of foreign objects. It is also important to note that each body has its own time schedule. It's not wise to compare your growth and timing to your friend's, sister's, or other females' growth. Some of our bodies will experience abnormalities (misshaped organ or breast, extra tissue in unusual places, excessive bleeding, unexplained pain, etc.). If this is you, tell a parent and/or seek medical attention immediately.

Body piercings and tattoos are popular in today's culture but can be dangerous if performed or applied by a nonprofessional. Give great consideration to the pros and cons of these practices. Consider the long-term effects as they relate to your overall health, relationships, career opportunities, and future of becoming a wife and/or mother. While there are techniques in place for removal should you change your mind after several years, know that the scarring will always be a reminder of their existence.

CARING FOR THE BODY

"Cleanliness is next to Godliness" -Phineas ben Yair

This section is intended to introduce you to the various ways to care for your body. It is not complete; therefore, you are encouraged to seek the advice of a parent and/or medical doctor for more information.

1. Cleanliness- There are numerous brands of personal care products on the market for use, but you should use care in selecting the ones that are right for your body and skin type, complexion, and allergies. Hair care products have special dyes and chemicals that can cause you to damage or lose your hair, so be sure to read the instructions and fine print that discuss the side effects. When all else fails, basic soap and water works just fine. Note that the vagina is a self-cleaning organ. If you detect a foul odor, burning, itching, or discharge you should consult a doctor immediately. Douches are unsafe and not recommended as they have a tendency to wash away healthy bacteria and may cause other problems.

2. Menstrual Cycle- The lower extremities will require extra attention during your cycle. Be sure to clean around your vaginal area each time you change your sanitary product. Monitor your clothing for staining. Change your sanitary products regularly to eliminate infections and/or unpleasant odors.

3. Infections- Infections may occur on or in the body. While some may be treated with over-the-counter medicines, others will require medical attention. Do not risk your health by ignoring or misdiagnosing yourself; seek medical attention right away. Refrain from all sexual activity

until you are mature enough to understand the ramifications of it. Oral and anal penetration is still a sexual act and is the cause of numerous life- threatening illnesses and diseases.

4. Diseases- Diseases are caused by many things: overeating, undereating, smoking, using drugs and/or alcohol, having sex with an infected partner, being exposed to toxic chemicals, etc. Don't allow others to entice you into doing anything that you know to be unhealthy. Today's pleasures become tomorrow's nightmares.

5. Mental Health- Our psyche has a lot to do with how we function from day to day. If we are not well mentally, then our physical health is affected. As we mature, we experience all sorts of emotions (love, hate, lust, fear, anger, shame, insecurity, loneliness, frustration, etc.). Mental abuse and rejection can add to or trigger these emotional symptoms. There are many ways to deal with these emotions, but because we lack the maturity, we will often choose the wrong methods. If you do not feel comfortable speaking with a parent, mentor, teacher, pastor, or other professional, there are hotlines available that offer you anonymity.

Talk to your parents, other responsible adults, or a medical professional about issues that concern you. Learn to walk away from situations that make you feel uncomfortable. If it causes you to lose a friend, then perhaps he/she was not a real friend in the first place.

DRUGS, ALCOHOL, AND SMOKING

Images of people smoking, using drugs, and drinking alcohol are all around you. You might even know somebody who has tried these things and thinks it is okay or cool. But the truth is, smart girls everywhere are saying "No, thanks." Be one of them! Girlshealth.gov can help by offering a lot of great information such as the following. In this section, you can learn

- What drugs do.

- How alcohol can hurt you.

- How to stay smoke-free.

- Important tips if you are already using drugs, alcohol, or tobacco.

You and your friends can support each other in avoiding drugs, alcohol, and tobacco. This is called positive peer pressure. Be strong for one another — that is what friends are for!

A lot of teens choose not to use drugs, alcohol, and tobacco or to misuse medicines. You can be strong like them! By saying "No!" to these things, you are saying "Yes!" to your health and your future.

WHAT ARE DRUGS

Drugs are chemicals that change the way your brain and body work. Drugs can be swallowed, inhaled, smoked, or injected. Whichever way you take drugs, they end up in your blood and go to all parts of your body.

Many drugs are illegal. That means it's against the law not just to sell them but also to have or use them.

The truth about illegal drugs

- Positive feelings from drugs wear off, but drugs can cause life-long damage to your body.

- Many drugs are addictive, which means it can be really hard to quit.

- Drugs affect the way you think, making it harder to make safe choices and protect yourself in dangerous situations.

- Drug use can lead to unhealthy sexual practices, such as having sex before you are ready or not asking if your partner has a sexually transmitted infection. Or, you may have sex without using a condom, which can put you at risk for getting pregnant or worse - HIV.

- Sharing needles and other equipment for injecting drugs can spread HIV and other dangerous infections.

- Drugs are not meant to be in your body. You could become real sick or maybe even die.

- Not only are drugs bad for your health, they can also change your looks dramatically! One of the effects that long-term meth users report is "crank bugs." A user may feel like there are bugs under her skin, so she keeps scratching at them until she Is scarred with sores and blisters.

WHAT'S THE DIFFERENCE BETWEEN "DRUGS" AND "MEDICINE"?

"Medicines" are what you take when you are sick or injured. Some, like the ADHD medications Adderall and Concerta, require a prescription from a doctor. Others are over-the-counter medicines, like aspirin or cough syrup, that you can buy without a prescription. The word "drugs" can be more confusing. Some people use it to mean illegal drugs that a doctor would never prescribe, like heroin or cocaine. Other people use it to mean both medicines and illegal drugs. For this segment, we use "drugs" to mean illegal drugs. Keep in mind, though, that prescription and over-the-counter medicines can be just as harmful—and deadly—as illegal drugs if you use them in ways that they are not meant to be used.

Be smart about prescription and over-the-counter medicines

Prescription medicines are ordered for you by a doctor to help with an injury or health problem. You may think that because doctors prescribe these medicines, they must be safe. Maybe you even think it is okay to pop some to stay awake or get high. But the truth is that prescription medicines can be dangerous if they are not used correctly. Check out these tips to stay safe:

- Always take prescription medicine in the way that your doctor tells you to.

- Never take someone else's prescription medicine or share your medicine with someone else. This is not safe, and it is not legal.

- Do not mix prescription medicines and alcohol. This mixture can be a deadly combination.

You don't need a doctor's prescription to buy over-the-counter (OTC) medicines. They are often used for basic problems, like colds and headaches. You can get them easily at pharmacies and grocery stores. But that does not mean they are always right for you. Be smart about OTC medicines:

- Do not take over-the-counter medicines without talking to your parent or guardian first.

- Always follow the directions on the package unless your doctor gives you other instructions. If you misuse them, some OTC medicines can be addictive and dangerous.

- Never use an OTC medicine to get high. Some young people have been doing this with cough and cold medicines that have dextromethorphan (also known as DXM or Dex) in them. This medicine is safe when used the way the package says, but if you take too much, you can throw up, have trouble breathing, and develop other serious problems.

- Also, be aware that people sometimes buy cold medicines that have pseudoephedrine in them to then make the dangerous illegal drug methamphetamine. This drug is highly addictive and can be deadly.

Drugs and medicines on the Internet

It is smart to avoid dangerous drugs and medicines no matter where they come from. However, buying on the Internet has its own special problems.

- Lots of online companies sell medicines, including over the-counter items you could get in a drugstore. Plenty of these companies are honest. Some, though, sell fake or unsafe medicines made with awful stuff like antifreeze. Make sure to talk to an adult before ordering online.

- Some websites will sell you prescription medicine even if you don't have a prescription. Others will sell you a prescription. Remember, prescription medicine is safe only if a doctor who knows you says it's right for you.

- You might be tempted to buy illegal drugs on the Internet. It can seem so private and easy. Don't be fooled, though. It Is always against the law to own these drugs.

KNOW WHEN THERE'S A PROBLEM

How do you know a friend has a problem with drugs? Your friend may

- Think drugs are the solution to all problems

- Spend a lot of time figuring out how to get drugs and how to get money to buy drugs

- Have unusual mood swings—she may be overly anxious, depressed, or irritable

- Have dropped out of regular activities and started hanging out with a group of drug-using friends

- Have stopped coming to school regularly

- Change her sleep habits

- Lose or gained a lot of weight

- Look sick, tired, or even messy

- Seem to be taking more and more of the drug to get the same effect

If a friend shows some of these signs, you can get help! Turn to your parents, teachers, counselors, or any adult you trust. Although you may be concerned about possibly getting your friend into trouble, the most important thing is to get help so that she can turn her life around—and maybe even save it.

If you think you may have a drug problem, do not let embarrassment or fear stop you from getting the support you need. There are a lot of ways to get help.

WHAT IS ADDICTION?

People sometimes toss around the word "addiction" and say things like "I'm addicted to chocolate." But what does it really mean to be addicted to drugs?

People who are addicted to a drug will have a strong urge or craving for it. In fact, they often will use lots of their time, energy, and money to get the drug. And they will do that even though they know the drug is hurting them—and even though they may be trying hard to stop.

What makes this happen? Usually, the decision to take drugs is a choice at first. But then the person's brain changes. It starts sending strong messages to take the drug and changes the person's ability to use self-control. The changes in the brain also can mean the person needs more of the drug to get the same effect, and it may mean that if they stop taking the drug, they have "withdrawal symptoms," or very uncomfortable feelings such as headaches and vomiting.

Addiction can be treated, though.

You are too strong, beautiful, smart,
and valuable to waste your life on drugs!

QUIZ

How smart are you about drugs?

Circle the correct answer for each question.

1. When the good feelings from a drug wears off, the danger to your body ends too.

   True   False

2. If you want to get high, which is safer?

   A. A friend's prescription medicine

   B. An over-the-counter medicine, like cough syrup

   C. A club drug, like ecstasy

   D. All of the above

   E. None of the above

3. What are some possible risks if you use drugs?

   A. Not being able to protect yourself in a dangerous situation

   B. Getting HIV

   C. Looking uglier

   D. Coma

   E. All of the above

4. You can buy drugs and medicines on the Internet easily and safely.

   True   False

5. Marijuana has over 400 chemicals in it.

   True   False

6. Some effects of the club drug ecstasy include:

   A. Upset stomach

B. Depression

C. Confusion

D. Anxiety

E. All of the above

7. Sniffing an inhalant like hairspray or paint thinner can cause brain damage.

   True   False

8. If a friend stops taking care of herself, starts skipping classes, or has sudden changes in mood, she may have a drug problem.

   True   False

QUIZ RESULTS

How smart are you about drugs?

1. When the good feelings from a drug wears off, the danger to your body ends too.

You answered false, which is correct! Drugs can cause damage that lasts long after the good feelings end. They can affect your memory and cause problems for your heart, lungs, and liver, for example.

2. If you want to get high, which is safer?

You answered e, which is correct! It's not safe to get high using any of these. Prescription and over-the-counter medicines may seem safer than street drugs because doctors give them or because they are easy to get. But prescription medicine is safe only for the person it is prescribed for — and only in the amount prescribed. Over-the-counter medicines can be addictive and dangerous if you take too much or misuse them in other ways.

3. What are some possible risks if you use drugs?

You answered e, which is correct! Drugs affect your mind, which means it can be harder to make safe choices and protect yourself. Drugs also can destroy your looks. For example, people who use the highly addictive drug methamphetamine often wind up with ugly scars. And drugs can cause an extreme reaction, like trouble breathing, coma, and even death.

4. You can buy drugs and medicines on the Internet easily and safely.

You answered false, which is correct! It is dangerous and against the law to use street drugs like LSD or cocaine anywhere you get them, including the Internet. The same goes for prescription medicines if they are not prescribed for you by a doctor who knows you.

5. Marijuana has over 400 chemicals in it.

You answered true, which is correct! Some people think marijuana is safe, but it can cause coughing and breathing problems just like regular cigarettes can. It also can cause memory loss, anxiety, and other serious problems.

6. Some effects of the club drug ecstasy include:

You answered e, which is correct! Drugs that people take at clubs can be dangerous.

7. Sniffing an inhalant like hairspray or paint thinner can cause brain damage.

You answered true, which is correct!

It is dangerous to sniff inhalants — even one time. You could have lots of problems, like fainting, vomiting, and even trouble breathing.

8. If a friend stops taking care of herself, starts skipping classes, or has sudden changes in mood, she may have a drug problem.

You answered true, which is correct!

Other signs of a problem with drugs are looking tired or messy, acting irritable or anxious, or sleeping more or less than before. Be a good friend and get your friend the help she needs.

HOTLINES FOR HELP

1. Access Mental Health http://dmh.co.la.ca.us
   (800)-8547771

2. DRUGS www.samhsa.gov/treatment/
   (800)-662-4357

3. GLBT National Help Center www.glnh.org/

4. National Center for Chronic Disease Prevention and Health Promotion www.cdc.gov/obesity

5. SUICIDE www.suicidepreventionlifeline.org/
   (800)-273-8255

6. DOMESTIC VIOLENCE www.thehotline.org/
   (800)-799-SAFE (7233)

7. RAPE AND SEXUAL ASSAULT www.rainn.org
   (800)-656-HOPE (4673)

8. ALCOHOL www.ncadd.org/
   (800)-622-2255 (888)-4AL-ANON

9. SEXUALITY AND RELATIONSHIPS plannedparenthood.org/info-for-teens/ (800)-300-108

10. EATING DISORDERS www.nationaleatingdisorders.org/ (800)-931-2237

CHAPTER THREE

RELATIONSHIPS

*R*elationships are a natural and necessary component for living. Relationships are defined as familial (mother, father, sisters, and/or brothers, etc.) and cultural (friends, classmates, neighbors, etc.) All relationships are important as they help us to grow into well-rounded individuals when all things are equal. In this generation, there are far too many dysfunctional families, but one person's dysfunction is another person's normal, so it is difficult to determine based on others' relationships what yours should be.

It is helpful if one has the benefit of having his or her mom and dad living in the home in a peaceful and loving setting, but when that is not the case, we must make the most of what we have. A familial relationship is compiled of all related parties (parents, children, step-parents, step-children, grandparents, uncles, aunties, etc.). All are responsible to the others in their respective roles. Each should warrant respect and demonstrate it in return.

Cultural relationships differ in that the responsibility is less restrictive. People can choose to what degree they will interact in these relationships, but they should always be respectful.

> *"If you judge people, you have no time to love them."*
> *- Mother Teresa*

GIRLFRIENDS

Girlfriends are very necessary at this stage in our lives. If we are lucky, we have at least one best friend. Good friends help us to be accountable and stay on track while some friends who don't necessarily have our best interest at heart will encourage us to engage in bad behavior. These are not true friends. They are called acquaintances and sometimes enemies (haters).

Here are 5 traits of a good friend:

1. Good friends will tell you the truth. They will be honest with you when it counts the most. Though it may hurt you at first, in the end, you will thank them for having your back.

ACCOUNTABILITY
♦ Accepting responsibility, behaviors, and attitudes
♦ Admitting mistakes (or being wrong)

TRUST
♦ Accepting each other's word
♦ Giving the benefit of the doubt

SAFETY
♦ Refusing to intimidate or manipulate
♦ Respecting physical space ♦ Expressing self nonviolently and honestly

RESPECT

COOPERATION
♦ Asking, not expecting
♦ Accepting change
♦ Making decisions together
♦ Being willing to compromise ♦ Seeking mutually satisfying resolutions to conflict

HONESTY
♦ Communication openly and truthfully

SUPPORT
♦ Supporting each other's choices
♦ Being understanding
♦ Offering encouragement
♦ Listening non-judgementally
♦ Valuing opinions

2. Good friends will be fun, unique, and interesting

They will cheer you up when you are sad or disappointed. They have something to share, and they will compliment your personality.

3. Good friends are attentive and supportive. They will know when you're in need of a good laugh or a hand with a project. They listen when you have something to say; they will even cry with you when needed.

4. Good friends care about you. They are concerned for your well-being; they will tell you when they think you're making a mistake, even if it means risking the loss of the friendship.

5. A good friend is consistent. A real friendship may experience some highs and lows but will last a lifetime.

"Good friends should build you up and never, ever tear you down."

MENTORS

Mentors are people who come into your life to teach you valuable lessons. Mentorship is learning and benefitting from someone else's experiences. Mentors can be a teacher, an older friend, or someone in your church, school, or sports affiliation.

There will be many relationships in your lifetime, but the best one is the one you have with yourself.

MY NEW BEST FRIEND

Today I met a great new friend
Who knew me right away,
It was funny how she understood
All I had to say
She listened to my problems
She listened to my dreams
We talked about love and life
She had been there, too, it seems

I never once felt judged by her
She knew just how I felt
She seemed to just accept me
and all the problems I'd been dealt

She didn't interrupt me
Or need to have her say
She just listened very patiently
And didn't go away

I wanted her to understand
How much this meant to me
But as I went to hug her
Something startled me

I put my arms in front of me
And went to pull her nearer
And realized that my new best friend
was nothing but a mirror
-Author Unknown

HEALTHY RELATIONSHIPS

In a healthy relationship, you and the other person talk honestly, listen well, and trust and respect each other. See below for info on each of these parts of a relationship. There are also some quick tips on how to build strong bonds below.

TALKING HONESTLY

- You feel comfortable sharing your thoughts, feelings, and experiences.

- Anything private you share stays just between the two of you.

- You feel comfortable asking what's up if the other person seems upset.

- You can talk through conflicts.

- Quick tip: Being honest usually is better than avoiding your feelings. When you try to ignore your feelings, they can pop back up in nasty ways.

LISTENING WELL

- You care about what the other person has to say.

- You avoid distractions and look straight at the other person (and not at your phone!).

- Even if you do not agree, you try to see the other person's side.

- Quick tip: Try repeating what you heard to make sure you understood what the other person meant.

TRUST AND RESPECT

- You feel valued for who you truly are—not surface stuff, like your clothes or looks.

- You can rely on the other person to keep promises.

- You trust the other person to understand if you make a mistake.

- You trust that the other person will support you through good times and bad.

- Quick tip: Try to show respect even when you argue. Later, I mention ways to handle conflict calmly.

GIVE AND TAKE

- You're assertive. You feel comfortable asking for what you want (and you do it respectfully).

- You are not aggressive. You do not try to get what you want by threatening or hurting the other person.

- You negotiate. That means both people trade ideas about what to do or how to handle an issue.

- You compromise. That means each of you gives up a bit of what you want to come to an agreement on an issue.

- Quick tip: Remember that parents sometimes set rules that are not open to negotiation. These are often rules made to keep you safe.

Want to build healthy relationships? You can start by connecting with—and liking—yourself. That way, you will know what makes you happy, and you'll know that you deserve to be treated well.

7 TIPS FOR HANDLING CONFLICT

Here are some smart steps to help you deal with conflict.

1. Cool off.
2. Keep it real!
3. Deal with the issue.
4. Listen to the other person's side.
5. Work it out.
6. Get help if you need it.
7. Walk away.

ARGUING WITH PARENTS OR GUARDIANS

Parents and teens disagree and argue at times, even though they love each other. Check out tips below for how to handle fights.

TIPS FOR HANDLING FIGHTS WITH PARENTS

- Talk about the rules. Ask the reasons behind a rule so you can understand it. Consider sharing how a rule makes you feel. Ask if your parents or guardians will consider your ideas about what the rules should be.

- Follow the rules. Keep to your curfew if you have one. Call if you're going to be late so your parents or guardians don't worry. If you follow the rules, your parents or guardians may be more likely to discuss them. If you don't follow the rules, you'll likely just get in trouble.

- Pick your battles. Cleaning your room is no fun, but it's most likely not worth fighting about.

- Spend time with your family. Some teens fight with their parents or guardians over how much time they spend with friends. Talk it over and make some special family time. You might go for a walk or have dinner together.

- Try to stay calm. Do not yell or stomp your feet when your parents or guardians say "no." If you listen and speak calmly, you may show them that you are growing up.

- After an argument, think about what happened. Consider your part in the problem, then apologize. Talk about how you might prevent similar fights in the future.

Source: GirlsHealth.gov

DOMESTIC VIOLENCE AND ABUSE

Domestic violence and abuse are used for one purpose and one purpose only: to gain and maintain total control over you. An abuser does not "play fair." Abusers use fear, guilt, shame, and intimidation to wear you down and keep you under their thumbs. Your abuser may also threaten you, hurt you, or hurt those around you. Another means of abuse is the withholding of things (money, food, clothing, gifts, etc.) from you.

Domestic violence and abuse do not discriminate; it happens among heterosexual couples and in same-sex partnerships. It occurs within all age ranges, ethnic backgrounds, and economic levels. And while girls/women are more commonly victimized, men are also abused—especially verbally and emotionally, although sometimes even physically as well. The bottom line is that abusive behavior is never acceptable, whether it is coming from a man, a woman, a teenager, or an older adult. You deserve to feel valued, respected, and safe.

There are many signs of an abusive relationship. The most telling sign is fear of your partner. If you feel like you need to walk on eggshells around your partner—constantly watching what you say and do to avoid a blow-up—chances are your relationship is unhealthy and abusive. Other signs that you may be in an abusive relationship include a partner who belittles you or tries to control you. These signs also include feelings of self-loathing, helplessness, and desperation. For more information on this subject, go to http://www.helpguide.org/articles/abuse/ domestic-violence-and-abuse.htm on the web, or speak with an adult, someone in whom you feel comfortable confiding

THE DATING GAME

At what age should you begin dating? This is a good question but is relative to certain factors. Dating is a serious act of engagement and can be defined in many ways such as talking on the phone; visiting in each other's home; meeting at a school or church function or going out independently together. One must prove that they are ready for each level of dating by being responsible, honest (trustworthy), and prepared.

a. Responsible - demonstrate ability to make sound decisions

b. Honest / Trustworthy - the ability to act on sound decisions. Do what you say you're going to do.

c. Prepared - the ability to discern when a problem exists and be equipped with the tools (fully charged cell phone, taxi fare, etc.) to handle it. Having the strength and courage to say "NO" and mean it.

LOVE AND SEX

As human beings, we have given ourselves or been labeled by many definitions, but only you know for sure who you really are. When in question, you should seek professional counsel for clarity. Living out who we really are may be somewhat challenging if who you believe yourself to be is different from the mainstream. To live your life for the purpose of pleasing others can be a very traumatic and self-destructive experience.

Love is supposed to be an emotion of joy; it should bring peace and pleasure, a sense of well-being. When love becomes painful, one should consider carefully the motives and value of the relationship.

I am no authority on this subject and therefore encourage you to seek additional information for a better understanding. The information provided here is simply to acknowledge the existence of these types of relationships:

Love- A strong feeling of affection and concern toward another person, as that arising from kinship or close friendship.

Sex - a) the classification of people as male or female, typically assigned at birth based on the appearance of external anatomy. b) physical activity in which people touch each other's bodies (kiss each other, etc.) that is related to and often includes sexual intercourse

Heterosexual - sexually attracted to people of the opposite sex

Cisgender - relating to someone whose sense of personal identity corresponds with the gender assigned to them at birth

Homosexual - sexually attracted to members of one's own sex

LGBTQIA - acronym for habits of those who do not adhere to the heterosexual and cisgender majority as follows:

> » Lesbian - a female homosexual, namely a female who experiences romantic love or sexual attraction to other females.

> » Gay - exhibiting sexual desire or behavior directed toward a person or persons of one's own sex.

> » Bisexual - is sexually attracted to males and females.

> » Transsexual - a person who strongly identifies with the opposite sex and may seek to live as a member of this sex.

> » Queer - an umbrella term for sexual and gender minorities that are not heterosexual. Originally meaning "strange" or "peculiar."

> » Intersex - an individual having reproductive organs or external sexual characteristics of both male and female.

> » Asexual - an individual who is not sexually attracted to either men or women.

Sources: Merriam Webster Dictionary, Free Dictionary, Urban Dictionary, Wikipedia

CHOOSING SOMEONE TO DATE

"Character speaks louder than promises." - Unknown

Most guys these days have been taught that because there are more females than males, girls are desperate and will accept anything. We must prove them wrong. We must demonstrate that we are worthy of so much more than to be treated as a passing fancy or hookup. With social/sexual diseases (STDs,

Aids) running rampant, we must do our homework to ensure that the guys we give our time to are worthy.

1. Know who you are.

2. Know what you want.

3. Know what you don't want.

4. Surround yourself with people who have qualities that compliment your own or who call you to a higher level. Never lower your standards.

5. Take the time to know the person before becoming intimate. If he deems you worthy, he will wait for you.

WHAT IF IT'S TOO LATE?

"I've already begun to date I did not apply your suggestions and now wear the label of 'used merchandise.' How can I redeem myself?"

While we cannot undo the past, we can make better choices for the future. Acknowledging your mistakes is the first step to creating a "New You." You now know who you don't want to be, so begin to recreate yourself using this knowledge:

1. Create a list of the characteristics you seek in the people you will date and stick to it.

2. Surround yourself with people who have qualities that compliment yours or calls you to a higher level. Never again lower your standards.

3. Take the time to know the next person before becoming intimate. As I mentioned earlier, if he deems you worthy, he will wait for you.

When you make these changes not only will you begin to feel better about yourself but also others will see the changes and regret that they did not treat you better.

> *"Be a girl with a mind, a woman with attitude, and a lady with class." -Unknown*

HOW DO I CHOOSE A BOYFRIEND?

Choosing a "boyfriend" is a serious step. It is one that should include careful consideration. Ask the question, why do I want a boyfriend now? Do I want a boyfriend or an acquaintance—just someone to hang out with? A boyfriend, ideally, is the prelude to a husband, so you should not go in search of him. He should find you. That is not to say that because a guy declares to you that he is the one, that you should just accept him. No, you should evaluate him based on his behavior with you and observe how he treats other girls. Remember, it takes time to know someone truly.

The person with whom you choose to be intimate, to cuddle, and to spend personal and private time with should be someone you respect and not just like. That person should be someone who respects you and genuinely wants to be with you.

This person should be able to carry his own weight financially when on a date. He should be a good conversationalist, a gentleman.

While, ideally, you can take care of yourself financially when on a date and when having your own transportation, the person who takes you on a date or becomes your boyfriend should lead by example and be equally or better equipped.

Do not be an enabler. Do not make excuses for someone who mistreats you, who disrespects you when in the presence of his or your friends. When you know that it is over, walk away.

Remember: How you start is how you will finish.

WHEN IS IT TIME TO GIVE IT UP?

*"A woman knows by intuition, or instinct, what is best for
herself."* -Marilyn Monroe

Give up what? Ok, if you really don't know, then that's a good thing. Age and maturity are truly relative when addressing this question. Notice that the quote above refers to a "woman"; a girl may not be so intuitive, and her instincts may not be so on point before she reaches age 18 which is one of the reasons age 18 is determined to be the age of maturity and consent for most.

The "what" has many names (cookie, cherry, nectar, peach, punani, puntang, coochie, cat, vajayjay, etc.); notice, they all have names that describe something sweet or special. That is because it is a girl's prized possession; it is what makes her special; it gives her power. So, we should not give it to just anybody. The man who receives this special gift or treat should be special himself, someone who possesses most, if not all, of the qualities of a husband.

Ideally, the first person to receive the honor of taking your virginity should be your husband because something special, though painful at first, will take place. It's a moment that should be shared with someone you love and not some immature boy who's only looking to add another feather to his cap and will move on to the next conquest the next day and share the news with his friends (homies). A real man feels like a king when he knows that he is your first.

If you share your virginity with someone other than your husband, you should be prepared that he may be a one-time wonder, so make sure that you are protected. Bring your own fresh condom and use it. This protection may not only protect you from an unwanted pregnancy but infections and diseases also.

Only you can know when the time is right. It should never be during your menstrual cycle or while you have an infection or STD. STDs (sexually transmitted diseases) can be contracted or transferred in ways other than penetration of the vagina. Foreplay is the first step, and it often will include oral (your mouth), especially among teens. Take time to google or read books on this subject to learn all the dangers that can be attributed to "just having a little fun." Oral and anal sex while they may prevent pregnancy, they cause so many other diseases, and since you don't know all of the partners your friend may have had before you, it's safe to just refrain all together.

Let the decision to give up your virginity be your decision and not someone else's. You do not have to go along with the gang when it is obvious that the gang does not have your best interest at heart. Popularity is relative; if it is popularity that you seek, then let it be for what's in your head and not for what's between your legs. What i's important is that you respect yourself enough to know when it's time to walk away.

"Too many girls rush into relationships because of the fear of being single, then start making compromises, and losing their identity. Don't do that." -Katy Perry

A word of caution: Do not be one of those girls who uses her charm to lure a boy and then become the target of his wrath when he's not allowed to have what he was offered or suggested. Boys/men take this kind of thing very seriously, and once they become "turned on," it is not easy for most to stop or walk away. So, when you play with fire, expect to get burned.

"A girl/woman is not written in braille. You don't have to touch her to know her." -Unknown

Every boy that comes along and tells you that you are pretty or that he likes you is not a candidate for the "cookie"; some are just shopping around to see who will say "yes." Take the time to develop a real friendship before giving it up.

WHEN A BOYFRIEND BECOMES A POTENTIAL SPOUSE

How will I know when a boyfriend is seeking spouse status? A boyfriend is a short-term commitment. He may or may not take the relationship seriously.

"Boys are like purses. You're always gonna have that one boy that you're always comfortable with and you know you'll always kind of like. That's your purse that you wear everywhere. Then you have that gorgeous bag that you want everyone to see you with but the gorgeous bag is usually obnoxious or costs a lot of money. Then you have those other purses that you really like but you really don't want to be seen with." -Lauren Conrad

A potential spouse is the one who has been around for a while and shows no sign of leaving; he has learned your quirks and strives to accommodate you; he has developed a serious relationship with your parents and introduced you to his (provided they are relevant). He has shared with you his hopes and dreams for the future and has included you in the picture.

A potential spouse makes you feel like his queen. You are his priority.

"You don't need a man to solve your problems, but a man that won't let you go through them alone."— Unknown It is not your responsibility to go in search of a spouse, He will find you, for, "when a man finds a wife he finds a good thing" (Proverbs.18:22—paraphrased). "A true man does not need to romance a different girl every night, a true man romances the same girl for the rest of her life."— Ana Alas   Your job is to make yourself ready for this true man. Know what you want but be willing to compromise. However, never accept abuse from anyone. Usually you can tell if someone is abusive by the way he behaves with others. Walk away from anyone who demonstrates road rage or cruelty to animals; these signs show that someone may have unresolved anger issues. If that person is you, then perhaps you should seek counseling prior to engaging in a relationship.

MARRIAGE

Marriage is not meant for everyone. It requires dedication, commitment, and, most importantly, true love to survive.

Marriage is intended to last until death, so one should be sure they are ready and willing to settle down with one partner.

One should never rush into marriage. You should take the time to know your potential mate and become comfortable with his idiosyncrasies.

Marriage is a sacred act and should not be entered into to try and fix a mistake such as an unplanned pregnancy. Most marriages that occur for this reason will end in separation and/ or divorce. A child deserves a happy and healthy home with parents who love each other.

When possible, before marriage meet the family of your potential spouse; learn who he really is. Generally, if he is good to his mother, he'll be good to you also.

Ask the hard questions: the "what ifs." Inquire about any medical or mental or financial issues with him or his family as well as any criminal behavior or history. Be ready to share your own. This does not have to be a deal breaker, but it helps to know what to expect for you and your future children.

Marriage to someone you adore and with whom you choose to spend the rest of your life with can be a wonderful thing. There is nothing more special than having a constant companion, friend, and lover who shares in your dreams, successes, and disappointments.

Marriage is between three people: you, your mate, and God; anyone else is one too many so be sure before you say, "I DO."

BECOMING A MOTHER Motherhood is a gift. Every young lady who births a child will not become a mother, and some mothers will have the pleasure of raising children that they did not birth.

Generally, a mother plans for the experience of motherhood. She has completed high school and maybe even college; she has cared for her body and has chosen a mate with whom to marry and father her child. For many, this is the fairy tale version. In reality, mothers come from all walks of life—they are very young without a plan, middle-aged, poor, illiterate, educated, single, and diverse in race, religion, and ethnicity. Motherhood is easiest when planned but is manageable otherwise with maturity and love.

Ideally, motherhood should never be entered into until one is ready. Motherhood is the result of sex between a boy and girl, man and woman. In most cases, it's an intentional act that should be carefully considered and reserved for marriage.

Becoming a mother forces one to grow up very quickly; it requires making sacrifices of time, energy, and pleasures. It is a physical, emotional, and financial responsibility. A very special bond is created between a mother and her child when all things are equal. When a child is born from one's body, no matter what happens after that, you're forever changed.

A healthy relationship produces a healthy and happy child. A healthy relationship is built on love, trust, and a faith in something greater than oneself.

CHAPTER FOUR

LIFE IS TOUGH - HOW DO I COPE?

*A*s we mature, our expectations change, and we feel challenged to change with them. We must become more independent; we think and work harder. We must learn how to interact with others on their terms, their level, and we must let go of the comforts we've come to enjoy from our parents, our siblings, and others.

As life evolves, we must change to keep up. This sometimes brings about a great deal of stress, especially if we have not used our growing up years wisely and learned the coping skills necessary to enter the next phase of maturity. There are times when we wish we could go back to being that little girl and have the privileges older more mature girls enjoy. A lot of the stress and frustrations stems from this conflicted state of mind. It looks easy to be grown-up but really its hard work, and if we force the maturity process along, we may create irreparable damage to ourselves and others.

Do not rush your life; take the time to enjoy each phase enjoying the experiences along the way, especially the good ones, and use the not so good ones as lessons, for they will aid you as you become older to make fewer mistakes. Learn to love yourself by getting to know yourself and accepting you for who you are. Never allow someone else to define you, and never conform to the behavior of others "just to fit in." Be the best "you" that you can be and watch others try to mimic you.

Usually when we try to fit into a mold that has been designed by someone else, we become stressed and overwhelmed. There are many ways to handle stress, and you should always, when possible, involve your parents in your daily life. They are usually your greatest resource, your biggest fans, and want only what is best for you although they may not demonstrate it in a way that's acceptable to you. When in doubt, talk it out with someone neutral, someone who is mature: a teacher, counselor, grandparent, mentor, or professional help from a psychologist who is referred by your family physician. Neither drugs, tobacco, sex, alcohol, nor violence is the answer.

AFTER A WHILE

After a while you learn the subtle difference between
Holding a hand and chaining a soul.
And you learn that love doesn't mean leaning.
And company doesn't mean security,
And you begin to learn that kisses aren't contracts
And presents aren't promises,

THE SECRET CODE OF GIRLS

And you begin to accept your defeats
With your head up and your eyes open
With the grace of an adult, not the grief of a child.
And you learn to build all your roads on today
Because tomorrow's ground is too uncertain for plans.
And futures have a way of falling in mid-flight
After a while you learn that even sunshine burns
if you get too much.
So, plant your own garden and decorate your own soul,
Instead of waiting for someone to bring you flowers.
And you learn that you really can endure...
That, you really are strong,
And, you really do have worth.
And, you learn, and you learn with every goodbye you learn.
Veronica A Shoffstall

HANDLING CHALLENGING TIMES

As teens, we can face some scary family issues, like illness, abuse, and divorce. Here are some ways to help you feel better should they happen to you.

Running away Are fights at home so bad that you are thinking of leaving? Running away can be dangerous.

Think of ways you can cope, like going for a walk, doing something creative, or talking to a friend. Stay away from things like drugs and drinking since they only make problems worse.

If you need support from outside your family, talk to a trusted adult such as a teacher, religious leader, or school counselor. You also can contact a 24-hour crisis line and a helpline for kids and teens.

Keep reading for information on coping in some specific situations.

- Do you take care of someone in your family? If you are taking care of a family member, it's important to get help. That might mean getting help handling tasks or getting emotional support.

- Think of people you trust. You might go to a school nurse or counselor or an adult relative. Your teacher also may be able to help, especially if you need more time to get your homework done or other kinds of school support.

- Are you struggling because your parents are getting divorced? Remember, divorce is never a child's fault. With time and support, you can adjust to the changes you're facing. If your parents are getting divorced, it's normal to feel grief. So much of your life may be changing, and you may not have much control over what happens. You may feel angry, sad, lonely, scared, and lots of other emotions. All of these feelings can take time to heal. There are many things you can do to feel better about a divorce. For starters, you can remember that divorce is never a child's fault.

- Talk to your parents about how you're feeling. Tell them what would make the divorce easier on you such as "their resisting the need to argue in your presence or to remember that you love them both and need them in your life." Get help from friends. You might also consider joining a support group for kids of divorcing parents. Your parents, school nurse, school counselor, or other adults can help you look for one. Also, see if you can think about any personal strengths that helped you in hard times before.

- Do you have a relative in the military? Having a relative in the military can be scary and upsetting. If you have a family member in the military, you may have losses even if your relative never gets hurt. You may miss your relative when that person is away or feel sad, worried, or angry a lot. And it can be hard to adjust when that person comes back.

- Ask about how things are going to change when your family member gets deployed. Find out about any new responsibilities or privileges you may have.

Try not to put your life on hold while your family member is deployed. Set goals and make plans for yourself.

- Figure out how and when you're going to stay in touch with the family member who is away.

- Keep track of important moments to share with your family member. Make a film, write a blog, or create a photo journal.

- Help your family keep up important traditions. Consider creating new ones.

- Connect with other people who can relate. You might seek a support group or even a camp for military kids.

- Spend special time together when your family member comes back. Keep plans simple, though. Expect it to take time for that person to fit back into home life.

- Is your family having money problems? You can not solve your family's money worries.

- Does your parent have a drug or alcohol problem? If your parent has an addiction, you may feel scared or worried. Talk to a school guidance counselor, coach, or trusted teacher. For those who attend religious services, a clergy member is also an option.

Few things in life are harder than the death of a close relative. "Grief" and "grieving" are used to describe the feelings a person has after a death or other loss. You also may feel grief after a really bad experience (sometimes called a trauma) like being attacked or your home's getting destroyed. That is because the experience has caused you to lose important parts of the way your life used to be.

Feeling grief is normal. Every person has her own reactions to loss. Here are some reactions you might have if you are grieving:

- Strong emotions such as sadness, anger, worry, or guilt

- Few or no feelings like you are emotionally numb

- Crying spells or feeling like there's a lump in your throat

- Physical reactions such as having stomach aches or not sleeping

- Spiritual reactions like feeling disappointed in your religion or feeling even more connected to it

Grief can go on for many months, but it should lessen over time. Everyone is different, but you should expect to feel at least a little better after a couple of months. If your grief doesn't get better over time, you may need the help of a therapist. Also, you should reach out for help without waiting if you have signs of depression. These signs include feeling worthless, having trouble functioning in your life, or thinking about hurting yourself.

How can I deal with grief? Grief can be hard to handle. If you're feeling grief after a serious trauma, like a violent attack, talk to an adult you trust and see if therapy may help you feel better. Check out the list below for other tips on handling grief.

Different people handle grief in different ways. Ways of handling grief include the following:

- Find comfort in good memories

- Stay busy to keep your mind off the sadness

- Talk about your loss

- Exercise every day

- Put your feelings into words or pictures

- Listen to music

GETTING ALONG WITH STEP-PARENTS

A new stepparent can bring up lots of feelings. Even if you like your stepparent, you may feel sad, worried, or upset at times. Here are some tips that can help:

- Accept your feelings. It is natural to have feelings like confusion, anger, and guilt when a parent remarries. Do not worry that there's something wrong with you if you have any (or all) of these feelings!

- Sort through your feelings. Keeping a journal might help. Friends who have gone through a similar situation may also be able to offer tips.

- Talk honestly. If you don't like any new rules or situations, ask calmly and respectfully about changing them.

- Get support from your parent or another trusted adult. Adults who care about you really want to help. If it seems too hard to turn to a family member, talk to another adult you trust. If you are struggling, a mental health professional like a school counselor can help.

- Try to spend time with your stepparent. This new person is going to be around, and chances are you will be happier if you can find his or her more positive sides.

Keep in mind that with patience—and some hard work—lots of stepfamilies end up feeling very close.   Source: GirlsHealth.gov

KEEP STRESS IN CHECK

Stress is the emotional and physical way in which we respond to pressure.

Stress can cause both mental and physical symptoms. The effects of stress are different for different people.

The mental (emotional) symptoms of stress include:

- Tension

- Irritability

- Inability to concentrate

- Feeling excessively tired

- Trouble sleeping

The physical symptoms of stress include:

- Dry mouth

- A pounding heart

- Difficulty breathing

- Stomach upset

- Headache

- Frequent urination

- Sweating palms

- Tight muscles that may cause pain and trembling

It is almost impossible to live without some stress. And most of us would not want to, because it gives life some spice and excitement. But if stress gets out of control, it may harm your health, your relationships, and your enjoyment of life. Source: ehealth med

See below some of the ways to handle stress:

1. Develop a spiritual practice (pray)

2. Meditate

3. Educate yourself

4. Exercise

5. Choose a hobby or sport and engage regularly

6. Listen to mellow music

7. Breathe (take slow deep breaths often)

8. Journal

9. Do not allow others to steal your joy, only you can control how you choose to handle your emotions.

People may say things to hurt us; they may do things sometimes unconsciously, to set us off. We must choose the best way in which to deal with it. We can become angry but only for a moment then consider the value of their actions; count the cost of your response—will it cause more harm or good? Is it better to simply walk away and allow the perpetrator to ponder his/ her actions? Or should I retaliate and create a bigger problem? Allow the situation to diffuse itself by simply taking a moment to breathe before responding.

The prayer below is given as a petition to our Heavenly Father (Higher Power); it has proven to be strength in times of weakness and insecurity. It is here to help you if you desire to use it:

> *"Our Father in heaven, reveal who You are. Set the world right; do what is best—as above, so below. Keep us alive with three square meals. Keep us forgiven with You and forgiving others. Keep us safe from ourselves and the devil. You're in charge! You can do anything You want! You're ablaze in beauty! Yes!" (Matthew 6:9-13 - translation from the Message Bible)*

As mere human beings, we are fragile in nature, subject to make mistakes, and become fearful when we are uncertain about things. A Higher Power is our keeper, our strength, our protector, our conscious. He/she provides a calming presence, a shield against the enemy. We have the choice to accept or reject His/her presence in our lives. Once accepted He/she will never leave us alone.

A PRAYER

I surround myself with toys at night
Just like a little child,
And yet my dreams are different now
With yearnings to be wild.
I pray to keep these two selves safe
Each night before I sleep
The child is protected by
The grown-up I'll soon meet.
It's hard to close my eyes sometimes
When deepest needs collide,
The search for self continues strong –
It pulls me like the tide.
Put prayers on my pillow, please,

So, I can tread the night
And wake up as the girl I am
To greet with you the light.

AFFIRMATION

I am God's child -- I am innocent.

I am God's creation -- I am beautiful.

I am God's gift -- I am generous.

I am God's hope -- I am faithful.

I am God's wisdom -- I am knowing.

I am God's laughter -- I am joyful.

I am God's love -- I am me. Both from Celia Straus—from Prayers on My Pillow

THE LOSING OF "US"

When an emotional injury takes place,
the whole body begins a process
as natural as the healing of a physical wound.
Let the process happen.
Trust that nature will do the healing.
Know that the pain will pass, and, when it passes,
you will be stronger, happier, more sensitive, and aware.

Mel Colgrove—How to Survive the Loss of Love

DEPRESSION: MANTRAS -VS- MEDICATION

Depression is a serious mental illness that for many years could only be treated with medication, and most often it is said that the medication can often be worse than the illness itself. Using Mantras is another way to derail the onset of depression.

Depression is a mood disorder that causes a persistent feeling of sadness and loss of interest. Also called major depressive disorder or clinical depression, it affects how you feel, think, and behave and can lead to a variety of emotional and physical problems. You may have trouble doing normal day-to-day activities, and sometimes you may feel as if life isn't worth living.

More than just a bout of the blues, depression isn't a weakness and you can't simply "snap out" of it. Depression may require long-term treatment. But don't get discouraged.

Depression feels better with medication, psychotherapy or other holistic methods like mantras.

Some specific features of Depression are:

- Anxious distress. You worry a lot about things that might happen or about losing control.

- Mixed features. You have both depression and mania -- periods of high energy, talking too much, and high self-esteem.

- Atypical features. You can feel good after happy events, but you also feel hungrier, need to sleep a lot, and are sensitive to rejection.

- Psychotic features. You believe in things that aren't true or see and hear things that aren't there.

- Catatonia. You cannot move your body normally. You might be still and unresponsive or have uncontrollable movements.

- Seasonal pattern. Your symptoms get worse with changes in the seasons, especially the colder, darker months.

What Are the Warning Signs of Suicide?

Anybody who thinks or talks about harming themselves should be taken very seriously. Do not hesitate to call your local suicide hotline right away. Call 800-SUICIDE (800-784-2433); 800-273-TALK (800-273-8255); or, for the hotline for the hearing impaired, call 800-799-4889. Or contact a mental health professional ASAP. If you intend or have a plan to commit suicide, and you cannot talk to a parent, best friend, mentor, or school counselor go to the emergency room right away.

For persons of most faith traditions, mantras are defined as groups of words that are considered sacred, having psychological and spiritual powers. They are terms used loosely to refer to a phrase repeated over and over, or whenever a painful emotion or thought surfaces. When we feel depressed and anxious, by uttering certain words several times daily, either upon waking and specific times throughout the day or spontaneously, as needed to bring about a sense of calm.

While it is good to develop your own mantras, ones that will appeal to your emotions, that make you feel safe and are able to calm you down. Here are a few that may prove helpful:

1. **It Will Get Better** - When you feel desperate, hopeless, or afraid, realize that it is a temporary feeling. Repeat the phrase, "*It will get better*" over and over several times. You don't have to believe it at that moment. It's in affirming that it's possible that you will begin to feel better.

2. **Let it Go** - This mantra is helpful when you're caught in obsessive thinking, such as when you find yourself playing a particularly distressing thought or scene over and over in your mind. Someone has made you angry, and you spend way too much time rehearsing the incident, and the many ways you might seek revenge. *Let it Go.*

3. **I Am Breathing In, I am Breathing Out** - At times, we may feel overwhelmed due the pressures of life, too much

going on in and around us. Thich Nhat Hanh, a Buddhist monk recommends that we *breathe* to restore our peace and calm; to bridge the gap between our body and mind during these times. We do this by "Mindful Breathing", with each breath in - acknowledge that you are breathing in and do the same when you breath out.

4. **I Am Enough** - Everyone at one time or another in their life has felt inadequate in some way.

    It is important to remind ourselves when we feel unworthy, that as a child of God, *I am enough*, because God says that I am, and that no matter what may be going on at the moment it does not define my value as a human being.

5. **May My Life Be Of Benefit To Others** - It is easy for us to become focused on ourselves and forget that we have a purpose for living, and that purpose is to serve others, and that sometimes that service is required when we feel least willing, due to our own suffering of illness or anxiety. Another phrase we could use would be, "*Make me an instrument of your* (God's) *peace*". You can transform your pain into compassion for others.

Another mantra, one that is my favorite is "**All Is Well**". It matters not how badly I may be feeling due to physical illness or emotional distress (anger, disappointment, fear, etc.) I make a personal declaration that *All Is Well*, and it's not long before it is. The situation may still be present, but my mental attitude about it is different

Sources: WebMD & MayoClinic.org

CHAPTER FIVE

EDUCATION

WHY IS EDUCATION SO IMPORTANT

> *"The smartest thing a girl/woman can learn is never to need a boy/man." -Demi Lovato*

*I*n times past, a woman could do little without a man's permission. Her role was to stay home, birth, and raise the children. She was not allowed to work and make her own money. Her education was limited to minimize her ability to compete with her male counterparts.

Knowledge is power! The more we learn, the more we know, and the more we know, the better we will grow into being a productive and valuable person and contributor to society.

School is our source for learning, starting with pre-school where we learn to interact with others. Our teachers are gifts to us; they are not just paid staff. Most teachers are operating in their gift— their purpose. They want to be in the classroom and want to see us achieve to our highest ability. We should take advantage of their knowledge and learn all that we can.

School is a stepping- stone to our life's journey, our career. We should begin setting goals in middle school and begin to implement them in high school to ready ourselves for college or other non-traditional (trade school, etc.) higher learning institutions. The higher our GPA, the greater the potential for securing financial assistance and attending our school of choice. Start early. Do your research for the best colleges/schools and their requirements for entry. Never settle for mediocrity.

Once you have a good education, no one can take it away from you.

Never stop learning—for when you stop learning, you die.

STEPS FOR GETTING INTO COLLEGE

Freshman Year

Get set for a great high school career. It's important to remember that what lies ahead is not just a four-year audition for college. Still, one should be thinking now about what admissions staffers will be looking for.

- Seek advice and teacher feedback: Ask someone you trust to help you map out your classes. Grades are important in ninth grade. But rigor is really key too, so don't just go for easy A's. If you get a bad grade, accept it as constructive criticism; really read (or listen) to your teacher's comments and figure out how to do better. Check in with older students or, if you have one, your peer mentor to get advice from upperclassmen.

- Read voraciously: Books, newspapers, magazines, blogs— choose what engages you and remember to look up unfamiliar words.

- Get involved: Not only are you developing talents and interests that will catch a college's eye, but also, school is more fun when you have activities to look forward to.

- Use social media wisely: Be responsible. What you post will follow you which could be a good or bad thing. Use social media productively, such as by building a website or tweeting about current events. The technological profile you build is a part of your narrative.

Sophomore Year

Now that you're no longer a rookie, your job is to evolve as a learner. Besides studying the material, take note of what your Teachers value and consider how you can learn more efficiently and better.

- Refine your route: Look ahead to which 11th and 12th grade courses you might be interested in taking and plan to work on any prerequisites.

- Challenge yourself, but wisely: Create a balanced schedule. You want to strive for the best possible grades, but overtaxing yourself is bound to be counterproductive. Stressed-out brains don't work well.

- Get some practice: Will you take the PSAT this year? You'll get a better sense of where you stand if you know what is on the test before you take it.

Also, consider whether an SAT subject test makes sense in the spring. If you're enrolled in an AP or honors course now, the timing may be good. The College Board makes practice versions. Take at least one.

- Put together a resume: Note your hobbies, jobs, and extracurricular activities. The resume is a living document and should evolve as your experience does.

- Make the most of your summer: Although lounging by the pool can be relaxing, it won't help you uncover your passion. Work, volunteer, play sports, or take a class. Find an activity that builds on a favorite subject or extracurricular interest. And keep in contact with your mentors, advisers, counselors, etc. They are all a part of your support system.

Junior Year

Your grades, test scores, and activities constitute a big chunk of what colleges consider for admission. Do your best in class and truly prepare for tests you take.

Junior year can also be a time to step forward as a leader in the world outside academics. Explore pursuits that interest you, not just because the exercise will look good on an application, but also because it allows you to flourish as a person.

- Ask for help: As Einstein allegedly said, insanity is "doing the same thing over and over again and expecting different results." If you feel stuck in your studies and in need of a breakthrough, ask teachers, parents, or friends for help in finding a new approach.

- Speak up in class: You will need to ask two junior-year teachers to write recommendations. They can't know you without hearing your thoughts, so make sure to contribute in class. In addition, your counselor will write a letter of recommendation, so visit the counseling office and make him or her a part of your growing network.

- Get enough sleep: The single most important thing you can do as a learner is to get enough sleep. The average 16-yearold brain needs more than eight hours of sleep to function at 100 percent, and that's exactly where you want to be.

- Plan your testing calendar: Grades come first. But test scores matter, too. Talk with your parents and guidance counselor about which tests to take, when to take them and how to prepare for them.

First up, the PSAT. If your 10th-grade scores put you in reach of a national merit scholarship, it might be wise to spend concentrated time prepping. Then take the SAT or ACT in winter or early spring.

Do not worry if you don't get your ideal score; you can try again.

The SAT subject tests are also an option for May or June in areas where you shine or in subjects you covered junior year.

- Get involved: It is great to be able to show you've worked hard, are dedicated to an activity, play well with others—and can lead them. Start an arts discussion group that goes to museum openings or be voted team captain.

- Start building your list: Once you have a handle on your test scores, talk to a counselor and start your list of target schools, reaches, and safeties. Make use of new technology and apps to aid your research. Explore college websites and resources like ed.gov/finaid and U.S. News' Best Colleges. Again, be mindful of your online presence and be sure to clean up your Facebook and Twitter accounts. These accounts might be viewed during the college application process.

- Make some college visits: Spring break and summer vacation are ideal times to check out a few campuses. Also try to attend college fairs and talk with the folks behind the tables. They can give you a feel for their school and some good future contacts.

- Write: Procrastination does not make for a good college essay. Aim to have first drafts done by Labor Day. Share them with an English teacher or counselor.

Senior Year

You made it. Well, not quite yet. This year will also be a one of hard work and continued preparation. Colleges do consider senior-year transcripts. They can and will rescind offers to students who slack off, so stay focused.

- Check requirements: You're in the final stretch, so don't veer off track. Make sure you're completing all of the requirements for graduation as well as course requirements of the colleges on your list.

- Finish testing and check the boxes: You're in the final stretch. If necessary, retake the SAT, ACT or subject tests if needed. The early fall test dates will give you time to apply early.

Also, make sure you're completing all graduation requirements as well as course requirements for your target colleges.

- Ask for recommendations and polish your resume: Early in the school year, ask two teachers who can offer different perspectives on your performance if they are willing to write a letter on your behalf. Choose teachers with whom you have a good relationship and who will effectively communicate your academic and personal qualities.

- Apply: Select a core group of schools to which you will apply and consider which deadlines (e.g., early decision, early action) are most appropriate. Fill out each application carefully and ask someone to look over your essays with a critical eye.

Check that your colleges have received records and recs from your high school, and have your SAT or ACT scores officially sent in. A month from the date you submit your application, call the college, and confirm that it is complete.

- Follow the money: Many colleges require that all your financial aid application forms be turned in by February, but the earlier the better.

- Make the choice: Explore the colleges where you have been accepted. Visit their campuses again, talk with alumni, attend an accepted student reception. Then confidently make your college choice official by sending in your deposit.

This story is excerpted from the U.S. News "Best Colleges 2016" guidebook, which features in-depth articles, rankings, and data.

CHAPTER SIX

CAREER -VS- PURPOSE

I f we are lucky, our career becomes our purpose. Our purpose is the gift(s) that we were given at birth. It (they) is the thing from which we achieve the most fulfillment. The thing that brings us the greatest joy. It is something that we do for others; something that provides a service, fulfills a need.

Our career is built around that purpose. It can be the most rewarding and yet may not produce the most money. Money is good for the exchange of goods and services—it buys us things. But it cannot buy our most innate need which is love of self and of others. A career is developed in small steps; it's a journey—one that will or should grow with us as we become more mature. Many have started by flipping burgers only to end up the manager or owner of their own franchise or restaurant. A mad dash to the top generally ends up with a lot of broken dreams.

A career does not preclude one from having a family; however, it will generally precede marriage and the starting of a family. A career, to most, is a sign of success, a personal achievement. Success is relative however, it is measured by the individual, one person may determine their success by the amount of money they make while another may determine it by the number of people they are able to help or the number of awards on their wall, letters behind their name or stars on their uniform. Your success might be the manner which, you keep your home, raise your children, and be a good companion to your spouse. Whatever you choose, do it to the best of your ability.

"There are always two choices, two paths to take, one is easy. And its only reward is that it's easy." -Author Unknown

WHO'S IN CHARGE OF YOU?

"There is no happiness without self-accountability." – Author Unknown

Do you know that when all is said and done, it is you who is ultimately responsible for the decisions that you make? We learn right from wrong early in life. Some of us have parents who are strict disciplinarians, and some have parents who are very lenient, who allow us to 'chart our own course.' We know innately right from wrong, and as we mature we learn how to push the boundaries; to test our parents, seeing how far we can go; how much we can get away with.

Accountability means that we are responsible for our own actions. If we choose to take the high road when making decisions, we are more apt to achieve success, to gain the approval of our elders (parents, teachers, etc.). However, if we try to cut corners, if we lie, steal, or cheat, then we achieve labels such as irresponsible and untrustworthy.

The decisions that we make in the early years will be the basis for how we're perceived as we become older. Adverse actions that are cute at ages 3-5 may be acceptable at ages 10 -12 but may get you arrested at age 15, and life will become more difficult for you after that. Some think that 'playing by the rules' is boring, that it makes one unpopular, but everything comes with a price, with consequences, and you're never too young to make good and right decisions. When in doubt, ask questions. Humility will take you a long way toward a long and profitable life.

Your parents' responsibility is to love you and to teach you godly principles; however, because of life circumstances, all parents aren't equipped with this knowledge and, therefore, can't pass it on to you. That's why we have to rely on what we know innately which is a fundamental rule that we learn very early as "the golden rule"—love others as we love ourselves; do unto others no more than we want them to do unto us. Be kind because its right to do, it may not always be easy, but in the end, it will work to your good.

Hold yourself to a higher standard, lead with purpose.

QUIZ

Chart Your Own Course

Who knows better than you who you are, what your goals are, where you hope to go? Answer the following questions, add additional sheets if needed:

1. What is your most favorite thing to do?

_____

2. If you could be someone famous, who would it be?

_____

3. What do you least like about yourself?

_____

4. What do you like most about school, what subject?

_____

5. What do you look for in a friend?

_____

6. How are you a good friend?

_____

7. How would your parents describe you?

_____

8. Do you like to read? If yes, what are you reading?

_____

9. What are your hobbies?

_____

10. Do you need the attention of a boy to make you feel special? _yes _no If yes, why?

_____

11. What makes you unique?

_____

HOW DO I PICK THE RIGHT CAREER?

The most important thing you can do when trying to choose a career is to pick one that is right for you. That means it needs to fit well with your interests, aptitudes, work-related values, and personality type. Why? If a career fits these criteria, there is a better chance you will be satisfied with it and enjoy your work.

Your first order of business is to learn as much as you can about yourself. If you think you know all there is to know, you will surely be surprised by what you will discover by going through a self-assessment. While you can find online resources to help you with this, the most efficient and effective way to do it—although usually not cheap—is to hire a career development professional, for example a career counselor or career development facilitator. He or she will use various tools to help you gather information about yourself and, based on it, provide you with a list of careers that are a good match.

If finances are an issue, don't let that keep you from getting the help you need. Check with your local public library since some offer career planning help or will be able to direct you to local agencies that do. Also check with local colleges and universities. Most have career services offices which may be open to members of the community. Programs that train career counselors often have students work with clients at no or a low cost to gain experience.

The self-assessment is not your final step in figuring out what career is right for you, but it is a great starting point to begin your quest.

Yes, you will have a list of occupations as a result, but not everything on it will appeal to you, and some of the occupations won't be feasible choices. But you will not know any of that yet because your next step in choosing the right career is still ahead. It will start with gathering information that will include getting a job description, learning about required training and education, and seeing what the outlook for the field is.

Why is any of this important? None of us, not even those who are well versed in the field of career planning, can know everything there is to know about all occupations. You may have some careers on your list about which you know nothing or little. You should at least get a brief description before you decide that a career is not right for you. You may learn something you didn't know.

Finding out about required education and training is important too. Let's say, for example, there's an occupation on your list but it requires a great deal of education before you can begin working. If you have neither the desire nor the resources to commit to something like that, it's not a good choice for you.

Likewise, neither is a career that requires little training when you have the inclination and ability to earn a college degree.

Finally, you will be doing yourself a great disservice if you don't look at job outlook. Investing time training for a career only to find out there are limited opportunities when you are ready to enter your field of choice will leave you having to start over.

When you have narrowed down your choices to just a few, then you should investigate even further, perhaps conducting some informational interviews with those working in the field. You can now make an educated decision.

Source—Career Planning About.com

CHAPTER SEVEN

CIVIC RESPONSIBILITY

*E*very one of us has a responsibility to our family, our community, and nation. There are many levels of maturity that we must achieve to become a mature adult.

For that reason, we should live each day with great expectation. We should seek to learn all that we can about life and living in a free society. While we are all free spirits, we still have a social responsibility to each other. No two people are exactly alike; therefore, we must learn to respect each other's differences.

There are many opportunities for us to become involved in our government. It starts in our own homes with the honoring and respect of our parents, sisters, and brothers; in our community as good neighbors; by respecting our elders and helping how and when we can; and by being good examples through peer mentorship. We should get to know the laws of the land and adhere to them and refrain from participation in illegal and adverse activity.

Participate in a civic project in your school or within your community or volunteer for projects that benefit the elderly or under-privileged. Learn to protest peacefully for issues that interest you and, when old enough, register to vote and then vote.

AN ATTITUDE OF GRATITUDE

"Be thankful for what you have; you'll end up having more. If you concentrate on what you don't have, you will never, ever have enough." -Oprah Winfrey

It is easy to look at what others have and compare it to what we have, but is it fair to do so? There Is a saying, "the grass is always greener on the other side." That saying is relative to so many things, but if we think about it for a moment, we come to realize that most often, it's just a saying. What's good for one person may not be so good for another; we may not want to put in the work required to achieve the same results and find in the end that it wasn't worth it after-all.

As a young lady, this example may seem a bit over the top, but if you learn this lesson now, you'll be so much better for it later on. Perhaps you're privileged to have all that you desire and don't care what's on the other side. If so, then good for you, but it's nearly impossible to have everything we want all of the time. Sometimes we have more than we need or want while someone else has neither. Sometimes having it all is still not enough; deep within there's still a void. That usually means the need is for something much more valuable than material things such as the newest toy, shoes, or outfit. Gratitude is an emotion of connectedness, which reminds us we are part of a larger universe with all living things.

An attitude of gratitude is the act of being thankful for what we have, for who we are, and for those whom we love and who love us. An attitude of gratitude is the practice of going beyond ourselves to share with others who may be less fortunate.

PROJECTS: IT'S A "PAY IT FORWARD" PARTY! FOR CHARITY

Everyone loves a party! Invite your friends over for a themed (ice cream social, slumber party, pool party, etc.) event. Ask each one to bring 1 or 2 things that they no longer wear (must be in like-new condition) for donation to a homeless shelter or school clothes closet.

Tools Needed: Snacks, large box, wrapping paper, scissors & glue, shopping bags

1. Text party invitation to friends

2. Decorate box with wrapping paper and place by the front door

3. Prepare light snacks for party

4. Enjoy party

5. Next day, sort clothing, fold neatly, place in shopping bags, and deliver to shelter or school.

6. Text a note to party guests thanking them for their donation and attending your party.

PROJECTS: "GRATITUDE" JAR

Tools Needed: Mason Jar, photo of self, 2 sticky note pads of different colors, pen tape or glue

1. Apply your photo on outside of jar, place jar on your nightstand or dresser with pen and sticky notes

2. At the end of each day take a sticky note and write one thing you did that day to make someone else feel good then fold and place in jar. Using the second colored pad, write one thing that someone said or did to make you feel special then fold and place in jar.

3. When the jar is filled, remove the notes, read them, then discard them and start over.

CHAPTER EIGHT

LEGACY

*L*egacy is about life and living. It Is about learning from the past, living in the present, and building for the future.

A legacy may take many forms—our children, grandchildren, a business, an ideal, a book, a community, a home, some piece of ourselves. We should live our lives so that our legacy reflects all that we hold most near and dear.

> *"Live with integrity and courage".*
> *-Susan V. Bosak*

CHAPTER NINE

ADDITIONAL RESOURCES

1. Teens Health from Nemours – http://teenshealth.org/ teen/ your_mind/relationships/healthy_relationship. html#

2. Girls Health – http://kidshealth.org/teen/sexual_ health/

3. Teens Web MD – http://teens.webmd.com/

4. MedLine Plus – https://www.nlm.nih.gov/medlineplus/ teenhealth.html

5. Girls Health – http://www.girlshealth.gov/relation-ships/ healthy/index.html

6. eHealth Med – http://ehealthmd.com/content/what-stress#ixzz3yViGgA9n

CHAPTER TEN

SELF-ESTEEM PROJECTS

W ith so many things going on around us and within us, it helps to have goals and a vision for our lives. The following projects will help you to stay focused:

SELF -ESTEEM CALENDAR:

A. Buy or create a blank calendar

B. Write down one interesting activity for each alternate day such as "go shopping" or "sketch something today" or "visit with friends today"

C. Every day visit your calendar and plan for upcoming activities.

D. Be sure to include your parents in your planning.

E. After each activity, write in your journal how you felt and what, if any, significant event occurred as a result of completing the activity.

F. Repeat this process each month, add more activities, and include your family in some of your activities.

CREATE A VISION BOARD

A. Tools: a poster board, magazines, markers, and glue

B. Choose from magazine pictures and text that represent what you want to happen in your life over the next 5 years. (career, clothing, travel, education, sports, etc.) cut them out and paste them on the poster.

C. Write a brief description of what you selected under or beside each clipping.

D. Hang the poster where you can see it daily and revise it as needed.

JOURNALING

Journaling is a way to not only record special thoughts but also help one to cope with life's challenges.

Journaling is encouraged as a daily activity; it only takes a few minutes and can prove to be a valuable tool later in life. Journaling is like keeping a diary but does not have to replace your diary. In your diary, you may want to record your most private thoughts, and you can also do that in your journal, but you may not have anything special to record on a regular basis.

With your journal you can use it as a Gratitude journal to record instances when you felt blessed by someone or something—a teacher who helped with a project, a friend who shared with you, or a special gift presented to you by a parent. It can also be used as a Grief journal where you record those unpleasant circumstances of the day or your Sports /extra -curricular journal which allows you to catalogue special techniques, successes, moments with friends, and or team members. You can use one journal for all these instances.

A journal helps to release bad energies such as anger, fear, frustration, or a sense of loss; it can also capture special moments of joy, compassion, and appreciation. The act of journaling opens the flow for peace and contentment. There is no limit to the content, it's your time to express your rawest emotion in a quiet and private manner. It can help you to formulate your thoughts for communication with others.

A journal does not become outdated; it grows with you; it is often a chronicle of your life from adolescence to adulthood.

You will find, as a part of this book, a journal with suggestions for various types of entries and many blank pages. You're encouraged to add additional pages or purchase other journals that fit your personality.

"THINKING OF YOU" POST CARDS

Think about how it makes you feel when someone does something nice to or for you. Now pay it forward by doing something nice for someone else. This is just one example but there are many simple and inexpensive ways to brighten someone else's day.

Tools Needed: white or colored postcard paper or stock paper, markers, crayons, pencil, scissors, stickers(optional), magazines, glue

1. Cut paper into 4 squares.

2. Use markers, pencils, and crayons to write something encouraging on each card specific for the person who will receive it.

3. Use stickers and/or magazine clippings (flowers, candy, smiley face, etc.) to decorate cards.

4. Hand deliver or place card where its sure to be found by intended party or place in an envelope and mail to those who are far away.

IN CONCLUSION

S haring this information with you is helping me also. It confirms for me the saying' "It's never too late to learn". In my own thirst for knowledge and wisdom and understanding I choose to seek out opportunities for learning everywhere I go and seek to surround myself with people who are going where I hope to be someday. I hope you, will see the value in doing the same. The internet is full of knowledge, both good and bad. Choose wisely, know that what you consume today will manifest itself later in your life.

I hope that you will share the Secret Code of Girls with others. Feel free to contact us and share your thoughts or learn more via our blog/podcast at www.MaeDixon.com, and learn more about how you are impacting communities when you purchase a book or other products via our organization – A Will & Way, Inc. at www.awillandway.org. We are also available to speak with you personally or at your youth or women's group. Church or other events.

The Book is available on our websites, Amazon.com, Barnes and Nobles and other major book distributors or ask for it at your neighborhood bookstore or gift shop."

ABOUT THE AUTHOR

*M*ae Dixon utilizes her gifts and talents to inspire and empower others. A native Floridian, she was educated in Escambia County. She chose a career of entrepreneurship at a very early age enabling her to be actively involved in community service while raising her children. She earned certifications in Clerical and Retail Sales from George Stone Vocational Tech; Certification in Real Estate from The University of West Florida; she's a graduate of the Florida Realtor Institute (GRI) and attended Pensacola State College for Business Administration.

Her career began as a retail clerk, and then co-owner of an air conditioning & heating business; she was an assistant district manager for H & R Block, owner of a Bookkeeping and realty company for almost 40 years. She founded a non-profit organization for survivors of domestic violence. She is also currently the owner of MAE Dixon, LLC, providing holistic transformation consultancy services for business owners, leaders and individuals.

A person who believes in giving her best in all that she does. Mae has served as a Florida Supreme Court Certified County Mediator, founding Board Member of the Citizen's Law Enforcement Liaison Group, President of the Community Drug & Alcohol Commission, Community Advisory Council member for International Paper Board Member – for Junior Achievement, Board Member for Children Services Center Mentor for Escambia County School System, Chairman for

Esc-Pensacola Human Relations Commission, member of Escambia County Zoning Board and Founder of A Will & Way, Inc. to name a few.

She has achieved many accomplishments and earned numerous honors and awards for her professional and community service, those include President of the Pensacola Association of Realtors, President of the Pensacola Bay Area Assn of Realtors, Realtor of the Year (Pensacola Assn of Realtors) Top Gun in Real Estate award for multiple years, Outstanding Business Women's Award – Pensacola Business Journal/Pensacola News Journal, General Chappie James Jr. Award for Business, Business Woman of the Year, Certificate of Excellence for Outstanding Achievement in Business from the Pensacola Women's Business Center, Inc. A White Rose Recipient from Favor House Inc. (Domestic Violence). As a Writer, she has been featured in numerous business publications and newspapers.

She is an Amazon Best Selling Author for her first published book "The Secret Code of Girls – The Ins and Outs of Being a Female", her second book is "Restored By Grace – A Journey Like No Other" and Teen Journals – "I Am Blessed and Highly Favored – My Personal Journal" and "I Lead With Authority Because I Can – My Journal".

Her greatest achievement is her two sons who are her greatest champions and her family. Mae also enjoy the love and support of numerous others that she has nurtured and mentored.

www.ingramcontent.com/pod-product-compliance
Lightning Source LLC
Chambersburg PA
CBHW051035030426
42336CB00015B/2893